This Book Belongs To

_____

_____

Scan This

Copyright © **PIXELART STUDIO**

Color Test

A quick word on coloring

Let your imagination run wild. It's not necessary to pick real life colors, pick whatever colors you like most. You can even mix coloring mediums on an image. Coloring and drawing is the perfect way to explore your creativity. All decision is yours and our ultimate coloring books aim to stimulate unlimited creativity and fantasy. Start on an image whatever you like. There's no wrong choice!

How to use this book!

All you need is a pencil, eraser and colors!
Draw lightly at first. Add details according to the diagrams, but don't worry about being perfect! Artists frequently make mistakes; they just find ways to make their mistakes look interesting. Don't worry if your drawings don't turn out the way you want them to. Just keep practicing! Sometimes drawing the same thing just a few times will help.

Now
Let's color

Color This Page

_____

Color This Page

Color This Page

Color This Page

Color This Page

Color This Page

Color This Page

Color This Page

Color This Page

Color This Page

Color This Page

Color This Page

Color This Page

Color This Page

Color This Page

Color This Page

Color This Page

Color This Page

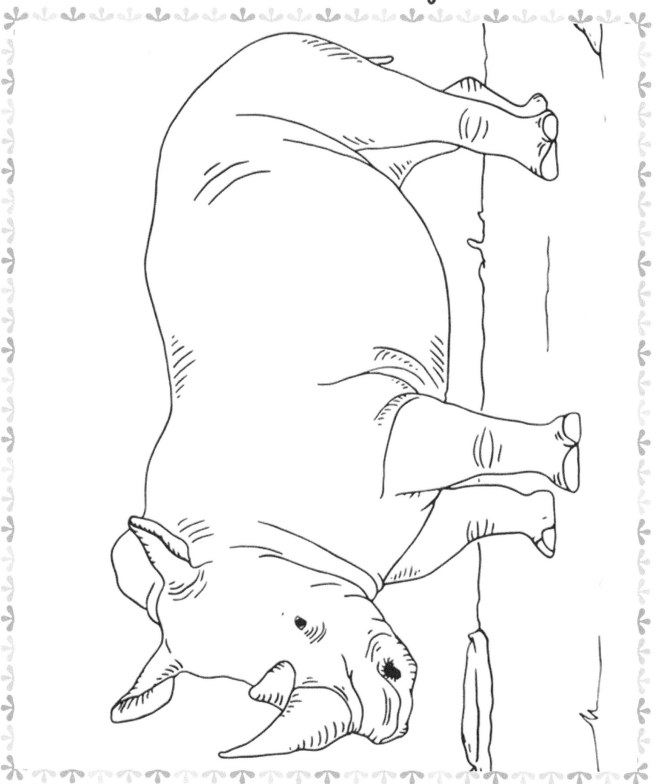

Color This Page

Color This Page

Color This Page

Color This Page

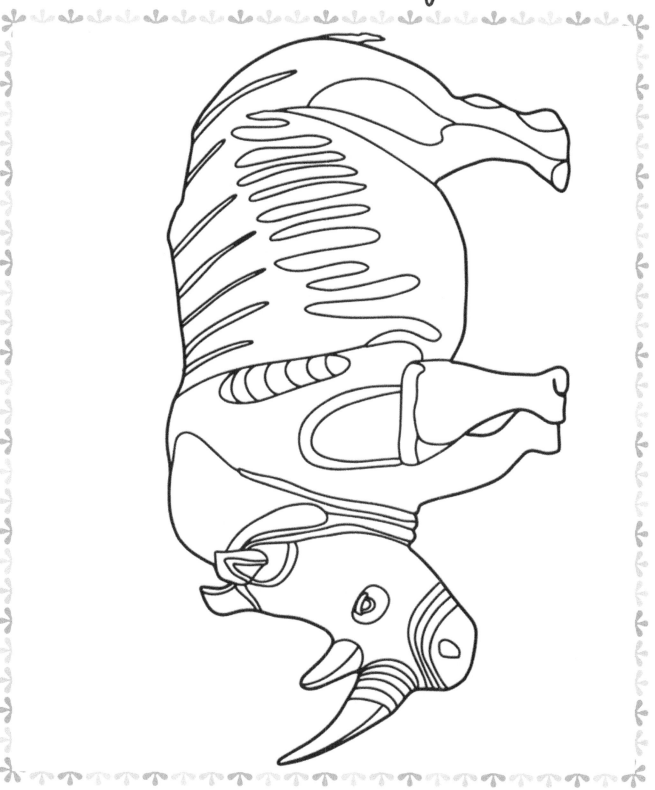

Color This Page

Color This Page

Color This Page

Color This Page

Color This Page

Color This Page

Color This Page

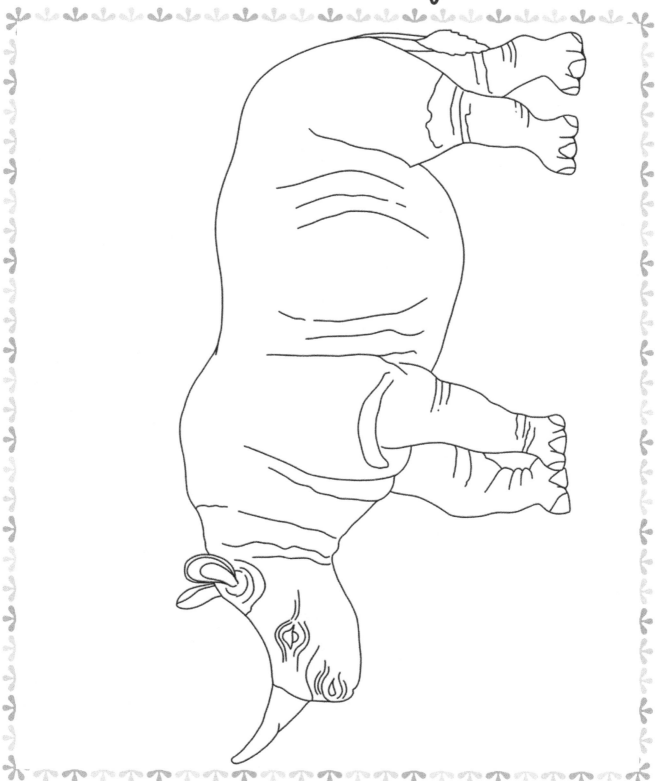

Color This Page

Color This Page

Color This Page

Color This Page

Color This Page

Color This Page

HEY!
WE WOULD LOVE
TO HEAR FROM YOU.

PLEASE LEAVE "*Pixelart Studio*" A REVIEW. YOUR FEEDBACKS AND OPINION CAN HELP US TO CREAT BETTER PRODUCTS FOR YOU.

COLORING BOOK..

Thank You!